24 HOURS ON THE SOMME

My Experiences of the First Day of the Somme, 1 July 1916

Edward Liveing

AMBERLEY

To the NCOs and men of No. 5 Platoon of a Battalion of the County of London Regiment, whom I had the good fortune to command in France during 1915–16, and in particular to the memory of RFN C. N. Dennison, my platoon observer, who fell in action on 1 July 1916 in an attempt to save my life.

This illustrated edition first published 2016

First published in 1918 as *Attack: An Infantry Subaltern's Impressions of July 1st, 1916*

Amberley Publishing
The Hill, Stroud
Gloucestershire, GL5 4EP

www.amberley-books.com

British Library Cataloguing in Publication Data.
A catalogue record for this book is available from the British Library.

ISBN 978 1 4456 5545 1 (print)
ISBN 978 1 4456 5546 8 (ebook)

Typesetting and Origination by Amberley Publishing.
Printed in Great Britain.

CONTENTS

Detail from a contemporary First World War propaganda poster showing soldiers on a battlefield setting up a machine gun. (Courtesy of Jonathan Reeve f239)

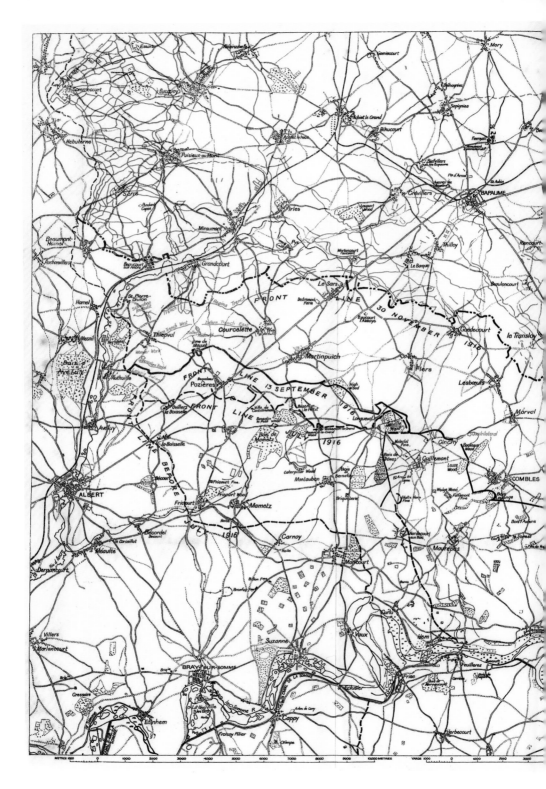

4

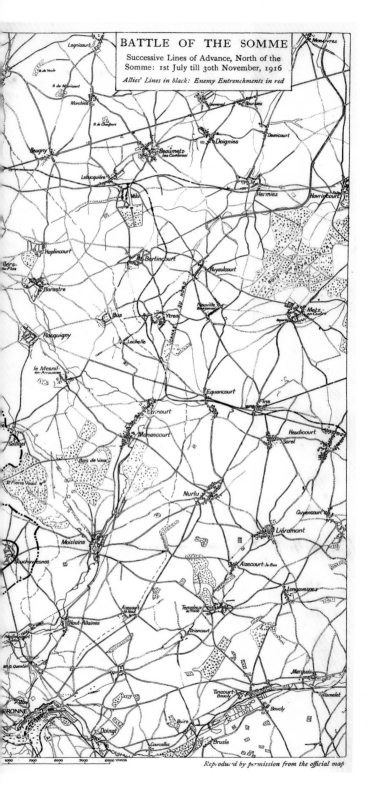

Map of the Battle
of the Somme,
1 July–30 November 1916,
showing successive lines of
advance. See top left quarter
for where Edward Liveing
was in action. (Courtesy
of Jonathan Reeve
b2000fp144)

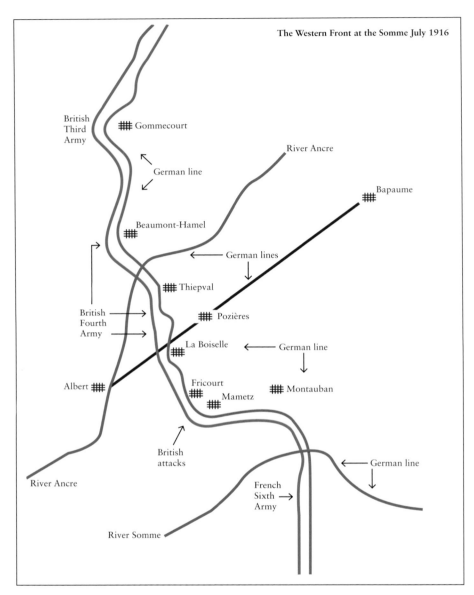

The Western Front at the Somme July 1916

British Third Army

Gommecourt

River Ancre

German line

Bapaume

Beaumont-Hamel

German lines

Thiepval

British Fourth Army

Pozières

La Boiselle

German line

Albert

Fricourt

Mametz

Montauban

British attacks

River Ancre

German line

French Sixth Army

River Somme

Map of the Somme sector of north-western France and designated for the July 1916 offensive. Blue depicts the Ancre and Somme Rivers, red the German front line and green the British and French front lines. The town of Bapaume was the overall British objective – a distance of less than 15 miles from the starting front lines. The towns of Mametz, Fricourt, La Boiselle, Montauban, Thiepval and Beaumont Hamel were all designated for conquest on Day One, but most would require four months of hard fighting to gain. The attack Edward Liveing fought in was aimed at the fortified village of Gommecourt. Bapaume was never reached. (Courtesy of Robert J Parker and the Amberley Archive)

1

GATHERING FOR ATTACK

The roads were packed with traffic. Column after column of lorries came pounding along, bearing their freight of shells, trench-mortar bombs, wire, stakes, sandbags, pipes, and a thousand other articles essential for the offensive, so that great dumps of explosives and other material arose in the green wayside places. Staff cars and signallers on motorbikes went busily on their way. Ambulances hurried backwards and forwards between the line and the Casualty Clearing Station, for the days of June were hard days for the infantry who dug the 'leaping-off' trenches, and manned them afterwards through rain and raid and bombardment. Horse transport and new batteries hurried to their destinations. 'Caterpillars' rumbled up, towing the heavier guns. Infantrymen and sappers marched to their tasks round and about the line.

Roads were repaired, telephone wires placed deep in the ground, trees felled for dugouts and gun emplacements, water pipes laid up to the trenches ready to be extended across conquered territory, while small-gauge and large-gauge railways seemed to spring to being in the night.

Then came days of terror for the enemy. Slowly our guns broke forth upon them in a tumult of rage. The Germans in retaliation sprayed our nearer batteries with shrapnel, and threw a barrage of whizz-bangs across the little white road leading into the village of Hébuterne. This feeble retaliation was swallowed up and

Above: Caterpillar tractors towing artillery on the Somme, 1916. (Courtesy of Jonathan Reeve b600p765b)

Below: British soldiers carrying long rolls of concertina wire move up towards the front line near Hamel during the Battle of the Somme. (Courtesy of Library of Congress)

Above: A British 18-pounder. The 18-pounder was the single most widely deployed gun on the Western Front by the British. (Courtesy of Jonathan Reeve B119pic30)

Below: A trench mortar. (Courtesy of Phil Carradice)

Above: A battery of 60-pounders. (Courtesy of Jonathan Reeve b600p860)

Below: A 15-inch howitzer being prepared for action, 1 July 1916, the Somme. (Courtesy of Jonathan Reeve b600p798t)

A 12-inch railway gun firing. A single 12-inch gun was used during the bombardment in advance of the launch of the attack on 1 July 1916. (Courtesy of Jonathan Reeve b600p752)

overpowered by the torrent of metal that now poured incessantly into their territory. Shells from the 18-pounders and trench mortars cut their wire and demoralised their sentries. Guns of all calibres pounded their system of trenches till it looked for all the world like nothing more than a ploughed field. The sky was filled with our aeroplanes wheeling about and directing the work of batteries, and with the black-and-white bursts of anti-aircraft shells. Shells from the 9.2 howitzers crashed into strong points and gun emplacements and hurled them skywards. Petrol shells licked up the few remaining green-leaved trees in Gommecourt Wood, where observers watched and snipers nested: 15-inch naval guns, under the vigilant guidance of observation balloons, wrought deadly havoc in Bapaume and other villages and billets behind their lines.

Above: A 6-inch heavy gun firing. Only twenty-four 6-inch guns were in use during the bombardment immediately before the launch of the attack on 1 July 1916. With two exceptions the 6-inch was the heaviest British gun available (as opposed to howitzers). The bombardment proved insufficient to achieve what the generals had planned: to destroy the German trenches, degrading the enemy troops to such a degree that the British Army could simply cross into No Man's Land and take the German trenches almost unopposed. (Courtesy of Jonathan Reeve b600p736)

Opposite: Douglas Haig, commander of the British army, with David Lloyd George and the French commander Joffre. In June 1916, Lloyd George, who had previously been Minister for Munitions, took on the role of Secretary of State for War following the death of Lord Kitchener; he would become Prime Minister in December 1916. (Courtesy of Library of Congress)

British troops marching past the Basilica of Notre-Dame de Brebières in Albert, three miles from the front lines of the Battle of the Somme. The statue of Mary and the infant Christ at the top of the tower was hit by a shell on 15 January 1915 and remained leaning until the tower was destroyed by shelling in 1918, becoming a familiar landmark to many British troops. (Courtesy of Library of Congress)

Thrice were the enemy enveloped in gas and smoke, and, as they stood to in expectation of attack, were mown down by a torrent of shells.

The bombardment grew and swelled and brought down showers of rain. Yet the ground remained comparatively dry and columns of dust arose from the roads as hoof and wheel crushed their broken surfaces and battalions of infantry, with songs and jests, marched up to billets and bivouacs just behind the line, ready to give battle.

2

EVE OF ATTACK

Boom! Absolute silence for a minute. Boom! Followed quickly by a more distant report from a fellow gun. At each bellowing roar from the 9.2 nearby, bits of the ceiling clattered on to the floor of the billet and the wall plaster trickled down on to one's valise, making a sound like soot coming down a chimney.

It was about three o'clock in the morning. I did not look at my watch, as its luminous facings had faded away months before and I did not wish to disturb my companions by lighting a match. A sigh or a groan came from one part of the room or another, showing that our bombardment was troublesome even to the sleepers, and a rasping noise occasionally occurred when WK, my company commander, turned round uneasily on his bed of wood and rabbit wire.

I plunged farther down into the recesses of my fleabag, though its linings had broken down and my feet stuck out at the bottom. Then I pulled my British Warm over me and muffled my head and ears in it to escape the regularly repeated roar of the 9.2. Though the whole house seemed to be shaking to bits at every minute, the noise was muffled to a less ear-splitting fury and I gradually sank into a semi-sleep.

About six o'clock I awoke finally, and after an interval the battery stopped its work. At half-past seven I hauled myself out of my valise and sallied forth into the courtyard, clad in a British Warm, pyjamas, and gumboots, to make my toilet. I blinked as I came into the light and felt very sleepy. The next moment I was on my hands and knees, with every nerve of my brain working like a millstone. A vicious 'swish' had

A dramatic image of artillery fire at night, the Somme, July 1916. (Courtesy of Jonathan Reeve B119pic63)

A 9.2-inch howitzer in action. (Courtesy of Jonathan Reeve b600p872)

sounded over my head, and knowing its meaning I had turned for the nearest door and slipped upon the cobbled stones of the yard. I picked myself up and fled for that door just as the inevitable 'crash' came. This happened to be the door to the servants' quarters, and they were vastly amused. We looked out of the window at the debris which was rising into the air. Two more 'crumps' came whirling over the house, and with shattering explosions lifted more debris into the air beyond the farther side of the courtyard. Followed a burst of shrapnel and one more 'crump', and the enemy's retaliation on the 9.2 and its crew had ceased. The latter, however, had descended into their dugout, while the gun remained unscathed. Not so some of our own men.

We were examining the nose cap of a shell which had hit the wall of our billet, when a corporal came up, who said hurriedly to WK, 'Corporal G's been killed and four men wounded.'

The whole tragedy had happened so swiftly, and this sudden announcement of the death of one of our best NCOs had come as such a shock, that all we did was to stare at each other with the words:

'My God! Corporal G gone! It's impossible.'

Detail from a contemporary First World War propaganda poster showing a 6-inch mark VII heavy artillery gun which was used during the Battle of the Somme. (Courtesy of Jonathan Reeve f237)

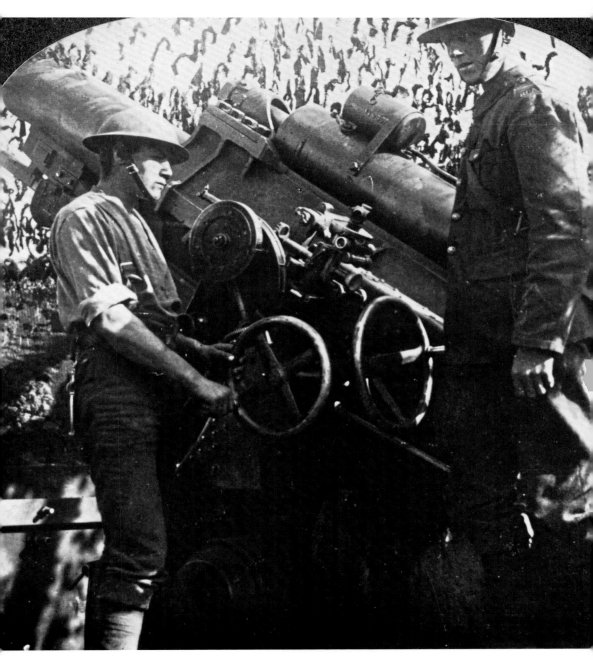

A British 9.2-inch howitzer under camouflage. (Courtesy of Jonathan Reeve JRf234)

One expects shells and death in the line, but three or four miles behind it one grows accustomed, so to speak, to live in a fool's paradise. We went round to see our casualties, and I found two of my platoon, bandaged in the leg and arm, sitting in a group of their pals, who were congratulating them on having got 'soft Blighty ones'. The company quartermaster-sergeant showed me a helmet, which was lying outside the billet when the shells came over, with a triangular gash in it, into which one could almost place one's fist. At the body of Corporal G I could not bring myself to look. The poor fellow had been terribly hit in the back and neck, and, I confess it openly, I had not the courage, and felt that it would be a sacrilege, to gaze on the mangled remains of one whom I had valued so much as an NCO and grown to like so much as a man during the last ten months.

A graphic image of German artillery firing, taken from a propaganda poster. (Courtesy of Library of Congress)

Dark clouds were blowing over in an easterly direction; a cheerless day added to the general gloom. We had a company officers' final consultation on the plans for the morrow, after which I held an inspection of my platoon, and gave out some further orders. On my return to the billet WK told me that the attack had been postponed for two days owing to bad weather. Putting aside all thought of orders for the time being, we issued out rum to the men, indulged in a few 'tots' ourselves, and settled down to a pleasant evening.

*

In a little courtyard on the evening of 30 June I called the old platoon to attention for the last time, shook hands with the officers left in reserve, marched off into the road, and made up a turning to the left on to the Blue Track. We had done about a quarter of the ground between Bayencourt and Sailly-au-Bois when a messenger hurried up to tell me to halt, as several of the platoons of the LS had to pass us. We sat down by a large shell hole, and the men lit up their pipes and cigarettes and shouted jokes to the men of the other regiment as they passed by.

It was a very peaceful evening – remarkably peaceful, now that the guns were at rest. A light breeze played eastward. I sat with my face towards the sunset, wondering a little if this was the last time that I should see it. One often reads of this sensation in second-rate novels. I must say that I had always thought it greatly 'overdone', but a great zest in the splendour of life swept over me as I sat there in the glow of that setting sun, and also a great calmness that gave me heart to do my uttermost on the morrow. My father had enclosed a little card in his last letter to me with the words upon it of the prayer of an old cavalier of the seventeenth century – Sir Jacob Astley – before the battle of Newbury: 'Lord, I shall be very busy this day. I may

Detail from a contemporary First World War German propaganda poster showing a burning British biplane plunging toward the ground. (Courtesy of Jonathan Reeve f240)

Artillery firing at night. Watercolour by Charles Meeres, whose artillery regiment took part in the bombardment on the eve of the first day of the Somme. (Courtesy of the estate of Charles Meeres)

forget Thee, but do not Thou forget me.' A peculiar old prayer, but I kept on repeating it to myself with great comfort that evening. My men were rather quiet. Perhaps the general calmness was affecting them with kindred thoughts, though an Englishman never shows them. On the left stood the stumpy spire of Bayencourt Church just left by us. On the right lay Sailly-au-Bois in its girdle of trees. Along the side of the valley which ran out from behind Sailly-au-Bois, arose numerous lazy pillars of smoke from the wood fires and kitchens of an artillery encampment. An English aeroplane, with a swarm of black puffs around it betokening German shells, was gleaming in the setting sun. It purred monotonously, almost drowning the screech of occasional shells which were dropping by a distant château. The calm before the storm sat brooding over everything.

Detail from contemporary British First World War propaganda poster *c.* 1915 showing artillery, most likely a BL 8-inch howitzer. (Courtesy of Jonathan Reeve f241)

The kilted platoons having gone on their way, we resumed our journey, dipping into the valley behind Sailly-au-Bois, and climbing the farther side; as I passed the officers' mess hut belonging to an anti-aircraft battery, which had taken up a position at the foot of the valley, and whence came a pleasant sound of clinking glass, a wild desire for permanent comfort affected me.

Bounding the outskirts of Sailly-au-Bois, we arrived in the midst of the battery positions nesting by the score in the level plain behind Hébuterne. The batteries soon let us know of their presence. Red flashes broke out in the gathering darkness, followed by quick reports.

To the right one could discern the dim outlines of platoons moving up steadily and at equal distances like ourselves. One could just catch the distant noise of spade clinking on rifle. When I turned my gaze to the front of these troops, I saw yellow-red flashes licking upon the horizon, where our shells were finding their mark. Straight in front, whither we were bound, the girdle of trees round Hébuterne shut out these flashes from view, but by the noise that came from beyond those trees one knew that the German trenches were receiving exactly the same intensity of fire there. Every now and then this belt of trees was being thrown into sharp relief by German star shells, which rocketed into the sky one after the other like a display of fireworks, while at times a burst of hostile shrapnel would throw a weird, red light on the twinkling poplars which surrounded the cemetery.

As we marched on towards the village (I do not mind saying it) I experienced that unpleasant sensation of wondering whether I should be lying out this time tomorrow – stiff and cold in that land beyond the trees, where the red shrapnel burst and the star shells flickered. I remember hoping that, if the fates so decreed, I should not leave too great a gap in my family, and, best hope of all, that I should instead be speeding home in an ambulance on the road that

Above: What was once a wood in the Somme, destroyed by shellfire and fighting. (Courtesy of Library of Congress)

Opposite top: A barbed wire entanglement in front of the German trenches undergoing maintenance. Note the men working on wooden planks balanced on the wire in order to reach further into the entanglement. (Courtesy of Library of Congress)

Opposite bottom: German trenches churned by the weight of British artillery fire. (Courtesy of Library of Congress)

Soldiers on the way to the front line, from a contemporary British propaganda poster. (Courtesy of the Library of Congress)

stretched along to our left. I do not think that I am far wrong when I say that those thoughts were occurring to every man in the silent platoon behind me. Not that we were downhearted. If you had asked the question, you would have been greeted by a cheery 'No!' We were all full of determination to do our best next day, but one cannot help enduring rather an unusual 'party feeling' before going into an attack.

Suddenly a German shell came screaming towards us. It hurtled overhead and fell behind us with muffled detonation in Sailly-au-Bois. Several more screamed over us as we went along, and it was peculiar to hear the shells of both sides echoing backwards and forwards in the sky at the same time.

Under the shelter of a sunken road, British soldiers with ammunition approach the front line of the Somme, 1916. (Courtesy of Jonathan Reeve B2000p117)

British infantry going up to the front line silhouetted against the battlefield. (Courtesy of Jonathan Reeve B119pic11)

We were about four hundred yards from the outskirts of Hébuterne, when I was made aware of the fact that the platoon in front of me had stopped. I immediately stopped my platoon. I sat the men down along a bank, and we waited – a wait which was whiled away by various incidents. I could hear a dog barking, and just see two gunner officers who were walking unconcernedly about the battery positions and whistling for it. The next thing that happened was a red flash in the air about two hundred yards away, and a pinging noise as bits of shrapnel shot into the ground round about. One of my men, S (the poor chap was killed next day), called to me: 'Look at that fire in Sailly, sir!' I turned round and saw a great, yellow flare illuminating the sky in the direction of Sailly, the fiery end of some barn or farm building, where a high explosive had found its billet.

We remained in this spot for nearly a quarter of an hour, after which RD's platoon began to move on, and I followed at a good distance with mine. We made our way to the clump of trees over which the shrapnel had burst a few minutes before. Suddenly we found ourselves floundering in a sunken road flooded with water knee-deep. This was not exactly pleasant, especially when my guide informed me that he was not quite certain as to our whereabouts. Luckily, we soon gained dry ground again, turned off into a bit of trench which brought us into the village, and made for the dump by the church, where we were to pick up our materials. When we reached the church – or, rather, its ruins – the road was so filled with parties and platoons, and it was becoming so dark, that it took us

A communication trench through a wood on the Western Front. The trench system was made up of front-line, support and reserve trenches. These three rows covered 180 to 450 metres of ground. Communication trenches were dug at an angle to those facing the enemy, and were used to move men, equipment and food supplies to and from the front. (Courtesy of Jonathan Reeve JRb1001fp268)

Above: Drawing of a communication trench by Charles Meeres. (Courtesy of the estate of Charles Meeres)

Below: British machine-gunners (wearing gas masks) on the Somme, 1 July 1916. The success of the German machine-gunners was a major reason for the huge loss of life among the British forces. (Courtesy of Jonathan Reeve b600p730b)

Above: Trench signs like the ones Liveing would have seen marking Boulevard Street, Cross Street and Woman Street. These are genuine boards brought back from the Western Front; most were made from packing cases. (Courtesy of Jonathan Reeve B601p424)

Below: Trenches and dead trees on the Somme. (Courtesy of Jonathan Reeve f242)

some time before we found the dump. Fortunately, the first person whom I spotted was the regimental sergeant-major, and I handed over to him the carrying party which I had to detail, also despatching the rum and soup parties – the latter to the company cooker.

Leaving the platoon in charge of Sergeant SL, I went with my guide in search of the dump. In the general mêlée I bumped into WK. We found the rabbit wire, barbed wire, and other material in a shell-broken outhouse, and, grabbing hold of it, handed the stuff out to the platoon.

As we filed through the village the reflections of star shells threw weird lights on half-ruined houses; an occasional shell screamed overhead, to burst with a dull, echoing sound within the shattered walls of former cottages; and one could hear the rat-tat-tat of machine guns. These had a nasty habit of spraying the village with indirect fire, and it was, as always, a relief to enter the recesses of Wood Street without having anyone hit. This communication trench dipped into the earth at right angles to the 'Boulevard' Street. We clattered along the brick-floored trench, whose walls were overhung with the dewy grass and flowers of the orchard – that wonderful orchard whose aroma had survived the horror and desolation of a two years' warfare, and seemed now only to be intensified to a softer fragrance by the night air.

Arriving at the belt of trees and hedge which marked the confines of the orchard, we turned to the right into Cross Street, which cut along behind the belt of trees into Woman Street.

Turning to the left up Woman Street, and leaving the belt of trees behind, we wound into the slightly undulating ground between Hébuterne and Gommecourt Wood. 'Crumps' were bursting round about the communication trench, but at a distance, judging by their report, of at least fifty yards. As we were passing Brigade Headquarters' Dugout, the brigade major appeared and asked me

British soldiers fixing scaling ladders to the steep sides of a trench prior to going 'over the top'. (Courtesy of Jonathan Reeve b119pic57)

the number of my platoon. 'Number 5,' I replied; and he answered, 'Good,' with a touch of relief in his voice – for we had been held up for some time on the way, and my platoon was the first or second platoon of the company to get into the line.

It was shortly after this that 'crumps' began to burst dangerously near. There was suddenly a blinding flash and terrific report just to our left. We kept on, with heads aching intolerably. Winding round a curve, we came upon the effects of the shells. The sides of the trench had been blown in, while in the middle of the debris lay a dead or unconscious man, and farther on a man groaning faintly upon a stretcher. We scrambled over them, passed a few more wounded and stretcher-bearers, and arrived at the Reserve Line.

Captain WT was standing at the juncture of Woman Street and the Reserve Line, cool and calm as usual. I asked him if New Woman Street was blocked, but there was no need for a reply. A confused noise of groans and stertorous breathing, and of someone sobbing, came to my ears, and above it all, MW's voice saying to one of his men: 'It's all right, old chap. It's all over now.' He told me afterwards that a shell had landed practically in the trench, killing two men in front of him and one behind, and wounding several others, but not touching himself.

It was quite obvious to me that it was impossible to proceed to the support trench via New Woman Street, and at any rate my company commander had given me orders to go over the top from the reserve to the support line, so, shells or no shells, and leaving Sergeant SL to bring up the rear of the platoon, I scaled a ladder leaning on the side of the trench and walked over the open for about two hundred yards. My guide and I jumped into New Woman Street just before it touched the support line, and we were soon joined by several other men of the platoon. We had already suffered three casualties, and going over the top in the darkness, the men had lost touch. The ration party also had not arrived yet. I despatched the guide to bring up the remainder, and proceeded to my destination with about six men. About fifteen yards farther up the trench I found a series of shell holes threading their way off to the left. By the light of some German star shells I discerned an officer groping about these holes, and I stumbled over mounds and hollows towards him.

'Is this the support line?' I asked, rather foolishly.

'Yes,' he replied, 'but there isn't much room in it.' I saw that he was an officer of the Royal Engineers.

'I'm putting my smoke-bombers down here,' he continued, 'but you'll find more room over towards the sunken road.'

Lewis gunners on the Somme, 1916. (Courtesy of Jonathan Reeve b2000p317)

He showed me along the trench – or the remains of it – and went off to carry out his own plans. I stumbled along till I could just distinguish the outlines of the sunken road. The trench in this direction was blown in level with the ground. I returned to WK, whose headquarters were at the juncture of New Woman Street and the support line, telling him that the trench by the sunken road was untenable, and that I proposed placing my platoon in a smaller length of trench, and spreading them out fanwise when we started to advance. To this he agreed, and putting his hand on my shoulder in his characteristic fashion, informed me in a whisper that the attack was to start at 7.30 a.m. As far as I can remember it was about one o'clock by now, and more of my men had come up. I ensconced them by sections. No. 1 section on the left and No. 4 on the right in shell holes and the remains of the trench along a distance of about forty yards, roughly half the length of the trench that they were to have occupied. At the same time I gave orders to my right- and left-hand guides to incline off to the right and left respectively when the advance started. I was walking back to my headquarters, a bit of trench behind a traverse, when a German searchlight, operating

Tommies in a front-line trench at night. (Courtesy of Jonathan Reeve 3d81)

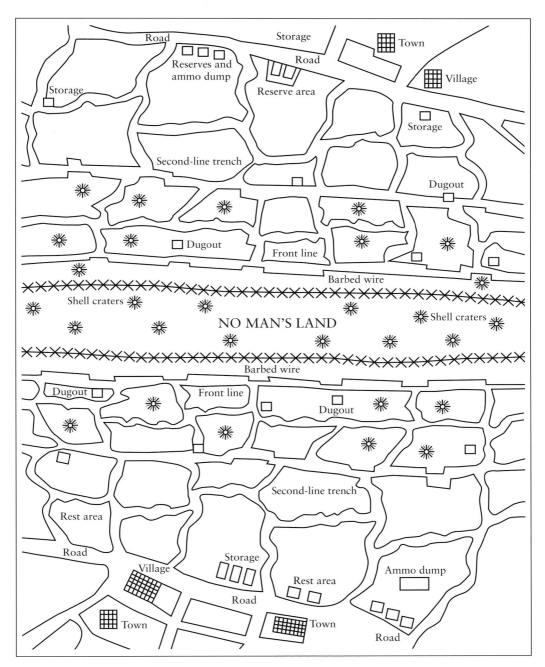

Diagram of a trench system. Front-line trenches are connected to second line/reserve trenches in case of retreat, and eventually wind back towards arterial roads, villages and towns. Connecting trenches provided access to front lines for rations, water, reinforcement and equipment. (Courtesy of Robert J. Parker and the Amberley Archive)

from the direction of Serre Wood, turned itself almost dead on me. I was in my trench in a second.

Shortly afterwards Sergeant SR arrived with No. 8 Platoon. I showed him one or two available portions of trench, but most of his men had to crowd in with mine. The Lewis-gunners, who arrived last, found only a ruined bit of trench next to my 'headquarters', while they deposited their guns and equipment in a shell hole behind.

It was somewhere about four or half-past when I made my last inspection. I clambered over the back of the trench and stood still for a moment or so. Everything was uncannily silent. There was just a suspicion of whiteness creeping into the sky beyond the rising ground opposite. Over towards the left rose the remains of Gommecourt Wood. Half its trees had gone since the last time that I had seen it, and the few that remained stood, looking like so many masts in a harbour, gaunt and charred by our petrol shells.

The men in the left fire bay seemed quite comfortable. But, standing and looking down the trench, it suddenly dawned upon me that I was gazing right into a line of chalky German trenches, and consequently that the enemy in those trenches could look straight into this trench. I left instructions with the corporal in charge of that section to build up a barricade in the gap before daybreak. As I went along the rest of our frontage, Sergeant SL doled out the rum.

I retired to my 'headquarters', but not so Sergeant SL, who seemed not to bother a bit about the increasing light and the bullets which came 'phitting' into the ground in rather an unpleasant quantity. I was glad when I had finally got him down into the trench. WK had also told him to get in, for he remarked, 'Captain WK, 'e says to me, "Get into the trench, SL, you b— fool!" so I've got in.'

He was just in time. A prelude of shrapnel screamed along, bursting overhead, and there followed an hour's nerve-racking bombardment.

3

ATTACK

Dawn was breaking. The morning was cool after a chill night – a night of waiting in blown-down trenches with not an inch to move to right or left; of listening to the enemy's shells as they left the guns and came tearing and shrieking towards you, knowing all the time that they were aimed for your particular bit of trench and would land in it or by it; of awaiting that sudden, ominous silence, and then the crash – perhaps death.

The front line on the Somme, 1916. (Courtesy of Jonathan Reeve B119pic27)

I, for my part, had spent most of the night sitting on a petrol tin, wedged between the two sides of the trench and two human beings – my sergeant on the left and a corporal on the right. Like others, I had slept for part of the time despite the noise and danger, awakened now and then by the shattering crash of a shell or the hopeless cry for stretcher-bearers.

A heavy shell exploding, Battle of the Somme, 1916. This photograph was taken by an official German photographer. Such shells were designed to blast trenches and barbed wire entanglements and kill and maim soldiers with razor-sharp and burning-hot shrapnel fragments. (Courtesy of Jonathan Reeve B119pic32)

But morning was coming at last, and the bombardment had ceased. The wind blew east, and a few fleecy clouds raced along the blue sky overhead. The sun was infusing more warmth into the air. There was the freshness and splendour of a summer morning over everything. In fact, as one man said, it felt more as if we were going to start off for a picnic than for a battle.

'Pass it down to Sergeant H that Sergeant SL wishes him the top o' the mornin',' said my sergeant. But Sergeant H, who was in charge of the company's Lewis guns, and had been stationed in the next fire trench, was at present groping his way to safety with a lump of shrapnel in his back.

An occasional shell sang one way or the other. Otherwise all was quiet. We passed down the remains of the rum. Sergeant SL pressed me to take some out of a mess-tin lid. I drank a very little – the first and last 'tot' I took during the battle. It warmed me up. Sometime after this I looked at my watch and found it was a minute or two before 6.25 a.m. I turned to the corporal, saying –

'They'll just about start now.'

The words were not out of my mouth before the noise, which had increased a trifle during the last twenty minutes, suddenly swelled into a gigantic roar. Our guns had started. The din was so deafening that one could not hear the crash of German shells exploding in our own lines.

Sergeant SL was standing straight up in the trench and looking over to see the effects of our shells. It was a brave thing to do, but absolutely reckless. I pulled him down by the tail of his tunic. He got up time and again, swearing that he would 'take on the whole b— German army'. He gave us pleasing information of the effects of our bombardment, but as I did not want him to lose his life prematurely, I saw to it that we kept him down in the trench till the time came for a display of bravery, in which he was not lacking.

Detail from a propaganda poster of a British field gun firing. (Courtesy of Jonathan Reeve f243)

Trench on the Somme, 1916. (Courtesy of Jonathan Reeve 3d47)

We had been told that the final bombardment that day would be the most intense one since the beginning of the war. The attack was to encircle what was most generally considered the strongest German 'fortress' on the Western Front, the stronghold of Gommecourt Wood. There was need of it, therefore.

Just over the trenches, almost raising the hair on one's head (we were helmeted, I must say, but that was the feeling), swished the smaller shells from the French .75 and English 18-pounder batteries. They gave one the sensation of being under a swiftly rushing stream. The larger shells kept up a continuous shrieking overhead, falling on the enemy's trenches with the roar of a cataract, while every now and then a noise as of thunder sounded above all when our trench-mortar shells fell amongst the German wire, blowing it to bits, making holes like mine craters, and throwing dirt and even bits of metal into our own trenches.

I have often tried to call to memory the intellectual, mental and nervous activity through which I passed during that hour of hellish bombardment and counter-bombardment, that last hour before we leapt out of our trenches into No Man's Land. I give the vague recollection of that ordeal for what it is worth. I had an excessive desire for the time to come when I could go 'over the top', when I should be free at last from the noise of the bombardment, free from the prison of my trench, free to walk across that patch of No Man's Land and opposing trenches till I got to my objective, or, if I did not go that far, to have my fate decided for better or for worse. I experienced, too, moments of intense fear during close bombardment. I felt that if I was blown up it would be the end of all things so far as I was concerned. The idea of afterlife seemed ridiculous in the presence of such frightful destructive force. Again the prayer of that old cavalier kept coming to my mind. At any rate, one could but do one's best, and I hoped that a higher power than all that which was around would not overlook me or any other fellows on that day. At one time, not very long before the moment of attack, I felt to its intensest depth the truth of the proverb, 'carpe diem'. What was time? I had another twenty minutes in which to live in comparative safety. What was the difference between twenty minutes and twenty years? Really and truly what was the difference? I was living at present, and that was enough. I am afraid that this working of mind will appear unintelligible. I cannot explain it further. I think that others who have waited to 'go over' will realise its meaning. Above all, perhaps, and except when shells falling nearby brought one back to reality, the intense cascade-like noise of our own shells rushing overhead numbed for the most part of the time one's nervous and mental system. Listening to this pandemonium, one felt like one of an audience at a theatre and not in the least as if one was in any way associated with it oneself.

Still, the activity of a man's nerves, though dulled to a great extent inwardly, were bound to show externally. I turned to the corporal. He was a brave fellow, and had gone through the Gallipoli campaign, but he was shaking all over, and white as parchment. I expect that I was just the same.

'We must be giving them hell,' I said. 'I don't think they're sending much back.'

'I don't think much, sir,' he replied.

I hardly think we believed each other. Looking up out of the trench beyond him, I saw huge, black columns of smoke and debris rising up from our communication trench. Then, suddenly, there was a blinding 'crash' just by us. We were covered in mud which flopped out of the trench, and the evil-smelling fumes of lyddite. The cry for stretcher-bearers was passed hurriedly up the line again. Followed 'crash' after 'crash', and the pinging of shrapnel which flicked into the top of the trench, the purring noise of flying nose caps and soft thudding sounds as they fell into the parapet.

It was difficult to hear one another talking. Sergeant SL was still full of the 'get at 'em' spirit. So were we all. The men were behaving splendidly. I passed along the word to 'fix swords'.

The effect of a trench mortar bomb explosion. (Courtesy of Jonathan Reeve B119pic6)

British soldiers 'fixing bayonets' prior to going 'over the top' during the Battle of the Somme. (Courtesy of Jonathan Reeve B2000p179)

Soldiers in a British trench 'fixing bayonets' before going 'over the top' on 1 July 1916 at the Somme. (Courtesy of Jonathan Reeve B2000p122)

Above: British troops going 'over the top'. Note the officer blowing his trench whistle. These were made in their tens of thousands and had the year they were made stamped prominently on the shaft. (Courtesy of Jonathan Reeve 3d83)

Opposite page: A 1916-issue trench whistle as used to signal the command to go 'over the top'. Edward Liveing doesn't refer to this in his memoir but they were used throughout the trenches on the first day of the Somme. (Courtesy of Jonathan Reeve f251)

We could not see properly over the top of the trench, but smoke was going over. The attack was about to begin – it was beginning. I passed word round the corner of the traverse, asking whether they could see if the second wave was starting. It was just past 7.30 a.m. The third wave, of which my platoon formed a part, was due to start at 7.30 plus 45 seconds – at the same time as the second wave in my part of the line. The corporal got up, so I realised that the second wave was assembling on the top to go over. The ladders had been smashed or used as stretchers long ago. Scrambling out of a battered part of the trench, I arrived on top, looked down my line of men, swung my rifle forward as a signal, and started off at the prearranged walk.

Soldiers going 'over the top', Somme 1916. (Courtesy of Jonathan Reeve B119pic64)

Above: Detail from a contemporary First World War propaganda poster showing Allied soldiers with bayonets charging through no man's land. (Courtesy of Jonathan Reeve f244)

Below: Dawn assault during the Battle of Somme. (Courtesy of Jonathan Reeve 3d55)

German machine-gunners. (Courtesy of the National Archives)

A continuous hissing noise all around one, like a railway engine letting off steam, signified that the German machine-gunners had become aware of our advance. I nearly trod on a motionless form. It lay in a natural position, but the ashen face and fixed, fearful eyes told me that the man had just fallen. I did not recognise him then. I remember him now. He was one of my own platoon.

To go back for a minute. The scene that met my eyes as I stood on the parapet of our trench for that one second is almost indescribable. Just in front the ground was pitted by innumerable shell holes. More holes opened suddenly every now and then. Here and there a few bodies lay about. Farther away, before our front line and in No Man's Land, lay more. In the smoke one could distinguish the second line advancing.

No man's land. (Courtesy of Jonathan Reeve f231)

No man's land. (Courtesy of Jonathan Reeve f232)

The toll of the Allied artillery: Germans dead in their pulverized trench. Despite the losses inflicted the British bombardment was far from sufficient to quell all resistance to the 1 July offensive. (Courtesy of Jonathan Reeve B119fpxvii)

One man after another fell down in a seemingly natural manner, and the wave melted away. In the background, where ran the remains of the German lines and wire, there was a mass of smoke, the red of the shrapnel bursting amid it. Amongst it, I saw Captain H and his men attempting to enter the German front line. The Boches had met them on the parapet with bombs. The whole scene reminded me of battle pictures, at which in earlier years I had gazed with much amazement. Only this scene, though it did not seem more real, was infinitely more terrible. Everything stood still for a second, as a panorama painted with three colours – the white of the smoke, the red of the shrapnel and blood, the green of the grass.

If I had felt nervous before, I did not feel so now, or at any rate not in anything like the same degree. As I advanced, I felt as if I was in a dream, but I had all my wits about me. We had been told to walk. Our boys, however, rushed forward with splendid impetuosity to help their comrades and smash the German resistance in the front line. What happened to our materials for blocking the German communication trench, when we got to our objective, I should not like to think. I kept up a fast walking pace and tried to keep the line together. This was impossible. When we had jumped clear of the remains of our front-line trench, my platoon slowly disappeared through the line stretching out. For a long time, however, Sergeant SL, Lance-Corporal M, Rifleman D, whom I remember being just in front of me, raising his hand in the air and cheering, and myself kept together. Eventually Lance-Corporal M was the only one of my platoon left near me, and I shouted out to him, 'Let's try and keep together!' It was not long, however, before we also parted company. One thing I remember very well about this time, and that was that a hare jumped up and rushed towards and past me through the dry, yellowish grass, its eyes bulging with fear.

We were dropping into a slight valley. The shell holes were less few, but bodies lay all over the ground, and a terrible groaning arose from all sides. At one time we seemed to be advancing in little

A dramatic photograph of soldiers in advanced positions just after going 'over the top' on 1 July 1916. (Courtesy of Jonathan Reeve JRb1001fp194)

groups. I was at the head of one for a moment or two, only to realise shortly afterwards that I was alone.

I came up to the German wire. Here one could hear men shouting to one another and the wounded groaning above the explosions of shells and bombs and the rattle of machine guns. I found myself with J, an officer of 'C' company, afterwards killed while charging a machine gun in the open. We looked round to see what our fourth line was doing. My company's fourth line had no leader. Captain WK, wounded twice, had fallen into a shell hole, while Sergeant SR had been killed during the preliminary bombardment. Men were kneeling and firing. I started back to see if I could bring them up, but they were too far away. I made a cup of my mouth and shouted, as J was shouting. We could not be heard. I turned round again

Barbed wire entanglements, the Somme, 1916. (Courtesy of Jonathan Reeve B119pic33)

German troops firing a machine gun from a prepared position on high ground. The German soldiers are still wearing pickelhaube helmets, which were phased out in favour of the more practical stahlhelm in 1916, starting during the Verdun campaign. (Courtesy of Library of Congress)

and advanced to a gap in the German wire. There was a pile of our wounded here on the German parapet.

Suddenly I cursed. I had been scalded in the left hip. A shell, I thought, had blown up in a waterlogged 'crump' hole and sprayed me with boiling water. Letting go of my rifle, I dropped forward full length on the ground. My hip began to smart unpleasantly, and I left a curious warmth stealing down my left leg. I thought it was the boiling water that had scalded me. Certainly my breeches looked as if they were saturated with water. I did not know that they were saturated with blood.

So I lay, waiting with the thought that I might recover my strength (I could barely move) and try to crawl back. There was the greater possibility of death, but there was also the possibility of life. I looked around to see what was happening. In front lay some wounded; on either side of them stakes and shreds of barbed wire twisted into weird contortions by the explosions of our trench-mortar bombs. Beyond this nothing but smoke, interspersed with the red of bursting bombs and shrapnel.

From out this ghastly chaos crawled a familiar figure. It was that of Sergeant K, bleeding from a wound in the chest. He came crawling towards me.

'Hallo, K,' I shouted.

'Are you hit, sir?' he asked.

'Yes, old chap, I am,' I replied.

'You had better try and crawl back,' he suggested.

'I don't think I can move,' I said.

'I'll take off your equipment for you.'

He proceeded very gallantly to do this. I could not get to a kneeling position myself, and he had to get hold of me, and bring me to a kneeling position, before undoing my belt and shoulder straps. We turned round and started crawling back together. I crawled very slowly at first. Little holes opened in the ground on either side of me, and I understood that I was under the fire of a machine gun. In front bullets were hitting the turf and throwing it four or five feet into the air. Slowly but steadily I crawled on. Sergeant K and I lost

German machine-gunners. (Courtesy of Jonathan Reeve b600p993T)

Above: German dead alongside a collapsed bunker during the Battle of the Somme.
(Courtesy of Jonathan Reeve B119pic59)

Above and opposite bottom: Bombing the Germans out of their deep dugouts during the advance on the Somme 1916. The results: a captured German is searched. (Courtesy of Jonathan Reeve 3d59 and 3d60)

German Stormtroopers. (Courtesy of Jonathan Reeve B119fp93 and B119fp93)

Dramatic contemporary illustrations showing the fighting on the Somme during July 1916. (Courtesy of Jonathan Reeve B2000p124 and B2000p146)

A dead German soldier. (Courtesy of Jonathan Reeve B119pic66)

sight of one another. I think that he crawled off to the right and I to the left of a mass of barbed-wire entanglements.

I was now confronted by a danger from our own side. I saw a row of several men kneeling on the ground and firing. It is probable that they were trying to pick off German machine-gunners, but it seemed very much as if they would 'pot' a few of the returning wounded into the bargain.

'For God's sake, stop firing,' I shouted.

Words were of no avail. I crawled through them. At last I got on my feet and stumbled blindly along.

Trenches pulverised by the British artillery barrage. (Courtesy of Jonathan Reeve b119pl46)

I fell down into a sunken road with several other wounded, and crawled up over the bank on the other side. The Germans had a machine gun on that road, and only a few of us got across. Someone faintly called my name behind me. Looking round, I thought I recognised a man of 'C' company. Only a few days later did it come home to me that he was my platoon observer. I had told him to stay with me whatever happened. He had carried out his orders much more faithfully than I had ever meant, for he had come to my assistance, wounded twice in the head himself. He hastened forward to me, but, as I looked round waiting, uncertain quite as to who he was, his rifle clattered on to the ground, and he crumpled up and fell motionless just behind me. I felt that there was nothing to be done for him. He died a hero, just as he had always been in the trenches, full of self-control, never complaining, a ready volunteer.

Royal Engineers signallers operating from a forward post in a shell hole. (Courtesy of Jonathan Reeve b119pl79)

Shortly afterwards I sighted the remains of our front-line trench and fell into them.

At first I could not make certain as to my whereabouts. Coupled with the fact that my notions in general were becoming somewhat hazy, the trenches themselves were entirely unrecognisable. They were filled with earth, and about half their original depth. I decided, with that quick, almost semi-conscious intuition that comes to one in moments of peril, to proceed to the left (to one coming from the German lines). As I crawled through holes and over mounds I could hear the vicious spitting of machine gun bullets. They seemed to skim just over my helmet. The trench, opening out a little, began to assume

Right: Detail from a contemporary First World War propaganda poster showing a wounded soldier having a field dressing applied to his wound. (Courtesy of Jonathan Reeve f245)

Below: Bringing in a wounded comrade after the opening attack of the first day of the Somme. (Courtesy of Jonathan Reeve b600p730t)

Opposite: Soldiers injured on the Somme, waiting for transport by ambulance, July 1916. (Courtesy of Jonathan Reeve b119pl74)

Right: The bringing in of wounded from the Somme battlefield under shellfire. (Courtesy of Jonathan Reeve b600p763)

its old outline. I had reached the head of New Woman Street, though at the time I did not know what communication trench it was – or trouble, for that matter. The scene at the head of that communication trench is stamped in a blurred but unforgettable way on my mind. In the remains of a wrecked dugout or emplacement a signaller sat, calmly transmitting messages to Battalion Headquarters. A few bombers were walking along the continuation of the front line. I could distinguish the red grenades on their arms through the smoke. There were more of them at the head of the communication trench. Shells were coming over and blowing up round about.

I asked one of the bombers to see what was wrong with my hip. He started to get out my iodine tube and field dressing. The iodine tube was smashed. I remembered that I had a second one, and we managed to get that out after some time. Shells were coming over so incessantly and close that the bomber advised that we should walk farther down the trench before commencing operations. This done, he opened my breeches and disclosed a small hole in the front of the left hip. It was bleeding fairly freely. He poured in the iodine, and put the bandage round in the best manner possible. We set off down the communication trench again, in company with several bombers, I holding the bandage to my wound. We scrambled up mounds and jumped over craters (rather a painful performance for one wounded in the leg); we halted at times in almost open places, when machine gun bullets swept unpleasantly near, and one felt the wind of shells as they passed just over, blowing up a few yards away. In my last stages across No Man's Land my chief thought had been, 'I must get home now for the sake of my people.' Now, for I still remember it distinctly, my thought was, 'Will my name appear in the casualty list under the head of "Killed" or "Wounded"?' and I summoned up a mental picture of the two alternatives in black type.

After many escapes we reached the Reserve Line, where a military policeman stood at the head of Woman Street. He held up the men in front of me and directed them to different places. Someone told him that a wounded officer was following. This was, perhaps, as well, for I was an indistinguishable mass of filth and gore. My helmet was covered with mud; my tunic was cut about with shrapnel and bullets and saturated with blood; my breeches had changed from a khaki to a purple hue; my puttees were in tatters; my boots looked like a pair of very muddy clogs.

The military policeman consigned me to the care of some excellent fellow, of what regiment I cannot remember. After walking, or rather stumbling, a short way down Woman Street, my guide and I came upon a gunner colonel standing outside his dugout and trying to watch the progress of the battle through his field-glasses.

'Good morning,' he said.

'Good morning, sir,' I replied.

This opening of our little conversation was not meant to be in the least ironical, I can assure you. It seemed quite natural at the time.

'Where are you hit?' he asked.

'In the thigh, sir. I don't think it's anything very bad.'

'Good. How are we getting on?'

'Well, I really can't say much for certain, sir. But I got nearly to their front line.'

Walking was now becoming exceedingly painful and we proceeded slowly. I choked the groans that would rise to my lips and felt a cold perspiration pouring freely from my face. It was easier to get along by taking hold of the sides of the trench with my hands than by being supported by my guide. A party of bombers or carriers of some description passed us. We stood on one side to let them go by. In those few seconds my wound became decidedly stiffer, and I wondered if I would ever reach the end of the trenches on foot. At length the communication trench passed through a belt of trees, and we found ourselves in Cross Street.

Here was a First Aid Post, and RAMC men were hard at work. I had known those trenches for a month past, and I had never thought that Cross Street could appear so homelike. Hardly a shell was falling and the immediate din of battle had subsided. The sun was becoming hot, but the trees threw refreshing shadows over the wide, shallow, brick-floored trenches built by the French two years before. The RAMC orderlies were speaking pleasant words, and men not too badly wounded were chatting gaily. I noticed a dresser at work on a man nearby, and was pleased to find that the man whose wounds were being attended to was my servant, L. His wound was in the hip, a nasty hole drilled by a machine gun bullet at close quarters. He showed me his water bottle, penetrated by another bullet, which had inflicted a further, but slight, wound.

There were many more-serious cases than mine to be attended to. After about five or ten minutes an orderly slit up my breeches.

'The wound's in the front of the hip,' I said.

Detail from a contemporary First World War propaganda poster showing a wounded soldier being stretchered away. (Courtesy of Jonathan Reeve f246)

'Yes, but there's a larger wound where the bullet's come out, sir.'

I looked and saw a gaping hole two inches in diameter.

'I think that's a Blighty one, isn't it?' I remarked.

'I should just think so, sir!' he replied.

'Thank God! At last!' I murmured vehemently, conjuring up visions of the good old homeland.

The orderly painted the iodine round both wounds and put on a larger bandage. At this moment R, an officer of 'D' company, came limping into Cross Street.

'Hallo, L,' he exclaimed, 'we had better try and get down to hospital together.'

We started in a cavalcade to walk down the remaining trenches into the village, not before my servant, who had insisted on staying with me, had remarked –

'I think I should like to go up again now, sir,' and to which proposal I had answered very emphatically –

'You won't do anything of the sort, my friend!'

R led the way, with a man to help him; next came my servant, then two orderlies carrying a stretcher with a terribly wounded Scottish private on it; another orderly and myself brought up the rear – and a very slow one at that!

Turning a corner, we found ourselves amidst troops of the battalion in reserve to us, all of them eager for news. A subaltern, with whom I had been at a Divisional School, asked how far we had got. I told him that we were probably in their second line by now. This statement caused disappointment. Every one appeared to believe that we had taken the three lines in about ten minutes. I must confess that the night before the attack I had entertained hopes that it would not take us much longer than this. As a matter of fact my battalion, or the remains of it, after three hours of splendid and severe fighting, managed to penetrate into the third line trench.

A contemporary illustration of a wounded soldier being carried into a first aid station by stretcher bearers, by Lucien Jonas, official war artist of the French Army. (Courtesy of Jonathan Reeve JRf230)

Loss of blood was beginning to tell, and my progress was getting slower every minute. Each man, as I passed, put his arm forward to help me along and said a cheery word of some kind or other. Down the wide, brick-floored trench we went, past shattered trees and battered cottages, through the rank grass and luxuriant wild flowers, through the rich, unwarlike aroma of the orchard, till we emerged into the village 'boulevard'.

The orderly held me under the arms till I was put on a wheeled stretcher and hurried along, past the 'boulevard pool' with its surrounding elms and willows, and, at the end of the 'boulevard', up a street to the left. A short way up this street on the right stood the Advanced Dressing Station – a well-sandbagged house reached through the usual archway and courtyard. A dugout, supplied with electric light and with an entrance of remarkable sandbag construction, had been tunnelled out beneath the courtyard. This was being used for operations.

In front of the archway and in the road stood two 'padres' directing the continuous flow of stretchers and walking wounded.

Bloodied soldiers are treated by an ambulance crew on the Western Front; a wartime illustration for the Red Cross fund. (Courtesy of the Library of Congress)

They appeared to be doing all the work of organisation, while the RAMC doctors and surgeons had their hands full with dressings and operations. These were the kind of directions:

'Wounded Sergeant? Right. Abdominal wound? All right. Lift him off – gently now. Take him through the archway into the dugout.'

'Dead? Yes! Poor fellow, take him down to the cemetery.'

'German? Dugout No. 2, at the end of the road on the right.'

Under the superintendence of the RC 'padre', a man whose sympathy and kindness I shall never forget, my stretcher was lifted off the carrier and I was placed in the archway. The 'padre' loosened my bandage and looked at the wound, when he drew in his breath and asked if I was in much pain.

'Not an enormous amount,' I answered, but asked for something to drink.

'Are you quite sure it hasn't touched the stomach?' he questioned, looking shrewdly at me.

I emphatically denied that it had, and he brought a blood-stained mug with a little tea at the bottom of it. I can honestly say that I never enjoyed a drink so much as that one.

Shells, high explosives and shrapnel were coming over every now and then. I kept my helmet well over my head. This also served as a shade from the sun, for it was now about ten o'clock and a sultry day. I was able to obtain a view of events round about fairly easily. From time to time orderlies tramped through the archway, bearing stretcher-cases to the dugout. Another officer had been brought in and placed on the opposite side of the archway. The poor fellow, about nineteen, was more or less unconscious. His head and both hands were covered in bandages crimson with blood. So coated was he with mud and gore that I did not at first recognise him as an officer. At the farther end of the arch a young private of about eighteen was lying on his side, groaning in the agony of a stomach wound and crying 'mother'. The sympathetic 'padre' did

Stretcher-cases awaiting ambulances during the Battle of the Somme. (Courtesy of Jonathan Reeve B119pic99)

Ambulances of the Royal Army Medical Corps picking up wounded. (Courtesy of Jonathan Reeve JRpc555)

the best he could to comfort him. Out in the road the RAMC were dressing and bandaging the ever-increasing flow of wounded. Amongst them a captive German RAMC man, in green uniform, with a Red Cross round his sleeve, was visible, hard at work. Everything seemed so different from the deadly strife a thousand or so yards away. There, foe was inflicting wounds on foe; here were our men attending to the German wounded and the Germans attending to ours. Both sides were working so hard now to save life. There was a human touch about that scene in the ruined village street which filled one with a sense of mingled sadness and pleasure. Here were both sides united in a common attempt to repair the ravages of war. Humanity had at last asserted itself.

It was about eleven o'clock, I suppose, when the 'padre' came up again to my stretcher and asked me if I should like to get on, as there was a berth vacant in an ambulance. The stretcher was hoisted up and slid into the bottom berth of the car. The berth above was occupied by an unconscious man. On the other side of the ambulance were four sitting-cases – a private, a sergeant, a corporal, and a rifleman, the last almost unconscious. Those of us who could talk were very pleased with life, and I remember saying: 'Thank God, we're out of that hell, boys!'

'What's wrong with him?' I asked the corporal, signifying the unconscious man.

'Hit in the lungs, sir. They've set him up on purpose.'

The corporal, pulling out his cigarette case, offered cigarettes all round, and we started to smoke. The last scene that I saw in Hébuterne was that of three men dressing a tall, badly wounded Prussian officer lying on the side of the road. The ambulance turned the corner out of the village. There followed three 'crashes' and dust flew on to the floor of the car.

'Whizz-bangs,' was the corporal's laconic remark.

We had passed the German road barrage, and were on our way to peace and safety.

4

TOLL OF ATTACK

We climbed the little white road which led through the battery positions now almost silent, topped the crest, and dipped into Sailly-au-Bois. The village had been very little shelled since the night before, and appeared the same as ever, except that the intense traffic, which had flowed into it for the past month, had ceased. Limbers and lorries had done their work, and the only objects which filled the shell-scarred streets were slow-moving ambulances, little blood-stained groups of 'walking wounded', and the troops of a new division moving up into the line.

Walking wounded. (Courtesy of Jonathan Reeve JRb600p731T)

Though we were all in some pain as the ambulance jolted along through the ruts in the side of the road, we felt rather sorry for those poor chaps as they peered inside the car. Our fate was decided, theirs still hung in the balance. How often on the march one had looked back oneself into a passing ambulance and wished, rather shamefully, for a 'Blighty' one. Sunburnt and healthy they looked as they shouted after us: 'Good luck, boys, give our love to Blighty!'

At the end of the village the ambulance swung off on a road leading to the left. It must have crossed the track by which my platoon and I had gone up the night before. About 11.30 a.m. we arrived at Couin, the headquarters of the First Field Ambulance.

A hum of conversation and joking arose from every side, and, with some exceptions, you could not have found such a cheery gathering anywhere. The immediate strain of battle had passed, and friends meeting friends compared notes of their experiences in the 'show'. Here a man with a bandaged arm was talking affectionately to a less fortunate 'pal' on a stretcher, and asking him if he could do anything for him; it is extraordinary how suffering knits men together, and how much sympathy is brought out in a man at the sight of a badly wounded comrade: yonder by the huts an orderly assisted a walking-case, shot through the lungs and vomiting blood freely.

Nearby I recognised E's servant of the LS. When he had finished giving some tea or water to a friend, I hailed him and asked him if Mr E was hit. Mr E, he told me, had been laid up for some days past, and had not taken part in the attack. He was, however, going round and writing letters for the men. Would I like to see him? We were fairly good acquaintances, so I said that I should. Presently he arrived.

'Bad luck, old chap. Where have you caught it?' he asked.

The remains of Gommecourt and Gommecourt Wood after July 1916. (Courtesy of Jonathan Reeve b600p804)

'In the thigh,' I replied.

He wrote two postcards home for me, one home and another to relatives, and I did my best to sign them. I remember that on one of them was inscribed: 'This is to let you know that E has been caught bending,' and wondering what my grandfather, a doctor, would make out of that!

The sun was beating down on us now, and since, after I had been duly labelled 'GSW (gun-shot wound) Back,' a medical staff officer advised that I should be transferred into the officers' hut, I entered its cooler shades with much gladness.

Captain WT came in soon afterwards. In the second-line German trench he had looked over the parados to see if any opposition was coming up from the third-line trench, and had been hit by a machine gun bullet in the shoulder. In making his way home he had been hit twice again in the shoulder. H also put in an appearance with a bullet wound in the arm. He had taken a party of 'walking wounded' up to Sailly-au-Bois, and got a car on. A doctor brought round the familiar old beverage of tea, which in large quantities, and in company with whisky, had helped us through many an unpleasant day in the trenches. Captain WT refused it, and insisted on having some bread and jam. I took both with much relish, and, having appeased an unusually large appetite, got an orderly to wash my face and hands, which were coated with blood.

'I dare say you feel as you was gettin' back to civilisation again, sir,' he said. Much refreshed, and quietly looking at a new number of the *Tatler*, I certainly felt as if I was, though, in spite of an airing, the wound was feeling rather uncomfortable. At the end of the hut two or three poor fellows were dying of stomach wounds. It was a peculiar contrast to hear two or three men chatting gaily just outside my end of the hut. I could only catch fragments of the conversation, which I give here.

'When Mr A gave the order to advance, I went over like a bird.'

'The effect of the rum, laddie!'

'Mr A was going strong too.'

'What's happened to Mr A, do you know?'

'Don't know. I didn't see 'im after that.'

"E's all right. Saw him just now. Got a wound in the arm.'

'Good. Isn't the sun fine here? Couldn't want a better morning for an attack, could you?'

The hut was filling rapidly, and the three stomach cases being quite hopeless were removed outside. A doctor brought in an officer of the Ks. He was quite dazed, and sank full length on a bed, passing his hand across his face and moaning. He was not wounded, but had been blown up whilst engaged in cutting a communication trench across No Man's Land, they told me. It was not long, however, before he recovered his senses sufficiently enough to walk with help to an ambulance. A 'padre' entered, supporting a young officer of the —, a far worse case of shell shock, and laid him out on the bed. He had no control over himself, and was weeping hysterically.

'For God's sake don't let me go back, don't send me back!' he cried.

The 'padre' tried to comfort him.

'You'll soon be in a nice hospital at the Base, old chap, or probably in England.'

He looked at the padre blankly, not understanding a word that he was saying.

A more extraordinary case of shell shock was that of an officer lying about three beds down from me. In the usual course of events an RAMC corporal asked him his name.

'F,' he replied in a vague tone.

The corporal thought that he had better make certain, so with as polite a manner as possible looked at his identification disc.

'It puts Lt B here,' he said.

There followed a lengthy argument, at the end of which the patient said –

'Well, it's no use. You had better give it up. I don't know what my name is!'

A Fusilier officer was carried in on a stretcher and laid next to me. After a time he said –

'Is your name L?'

I replied affirmatively.

'Don't you recognise me?' he questioned.

I looked at him, but could not think where I had seen him before.

'My name's D. I was your company quartermaster-sergeant in the Second Battalion.' Then I remembered him, though it had been hard to recognise him in officer's uniform, blood-stained and tattered at that. We compared notes of our experiences since I had left the second line of my battalion in England nearly a year before, until, soon afterwards, he was taken out to an ambulance.

At the other end of the hut it was just possible to see an officer tossing to and fro deliriously on a stretcher. I use the word 'deliriously', though he was probably another case of shell shock. He was wounded also, judging by the bandages which swathed the middle part of his body. The poor fellow thought that he was still fighting, and every now and again broke out like this –

'Keep 'em off, boys. Keep 'em off. Give me a bomb, sergeant. Get down! My God! I'm hit. Put some more of those sandbags on the barricade. These damned shells! Can I stand it any longer? Come on, boys. Come along, sergeant! We must go for them. Oh! My God! I must stick it!'

After a time the cries became fainter, and the stretcher was taken out.

About three o'clock I managed to get a doctor to inject me with anti-tetanus. I confess that I was rather anxious about getting this done, for in crawling back across No Man's Land my wound had been covered with mud and dirt. The orderly, who put on the iodine, told me that the German artillery was sending shrapnel over the ridge. This was rather disconcerting, but, accustomed as I had become to shrapnel at close quarters, the sounds seemed so distant that I did not bother more about them.

It must have been about four o'clock when my stretcher was picked up and I passed once again into the warm sunlight. Outside an orderly relieved me of my steel and gas helmets, in much the same way as the collector takes your ticket when you pass through the gates of a London terminus in a taxi. Once more the stretcher was slid into an ambulance, and I found myself in company with a young subaltern of the Ks. He was very cheery, and continued to assert that we should all be in 'Blighty' in a day or two's time. When the ASC driver appeared at the entrance of the car and confirmed our friend's opinion, I began to entertain the most glorious visions of the morrow – visions which I need hardly say did not come true.

'How were you hit?' I asked the officer of the Ks.

'I got a machine gun bullet in the pit of the stomach while digging that communication trench into No Man's Land. It's been pretty bad, but the pain's going now, and I think I shall be all right.'

Then he recognised the man on the stretcher above me.

'Hullo, laddie,' he said. 'What have they done to you?'

'I've been hit in the left wrist and the leg, sir. I hope you aren't very bad.'

The engine started, and we set off on our journey to the Casualty Clearing Station. For the last time we passed the villages, which we had come to know so intimately in the past two months during rest from the trenches. There was Souastre, where one had spent pleasant evenings at the Divisional Theatre; St Amand with its open square in front of the church, the meeting place of the villagers, now deserted save for two or three soldiers; Gaudiempré, the headquarters of an Army Service Corps park, with its lines of roughly made stables. At one part of the journey a 15-inch gun let fly just over the road. We had endured quite enough noise for that day, and I was glad that it did not occur again. From a rather tortuous course through by-lanes we turned into the main Arras to Doullens road – that long, straight, typical French highway with its avenue of poplars. Shortly afterwards the ambulance drew up outside the Casualty Clearing Station.

The Casualty Clearing Station was situated in the grounds of a château. I believe that the château itself was used as a hospital for those cases which were too bad to be moved farther. We were taken into a long, cement-floored building, and laid down in a line of stretchers which ran almost from the doorway up to a screen at the end of the room, behind which dressings and operations were taking place. On my right was the officer of the Ks, still fairly cheery, though in a certain amount of pain; on my left lay a rifleman hit in the chest, and very grey about the face; I remember that, as I looked at him, I compared the colour of his face with that of the stomach cases I had seen. A stomach case, as far as I can remember, has an ashen pallor about the face; a lung case has a haggard grey look. Next to him a boy of about eighteen was sitting

An anti-aircraft gun, or 'Archie' as they were better known, in action. (Courtesy of Jonathan Reeve JRf235)

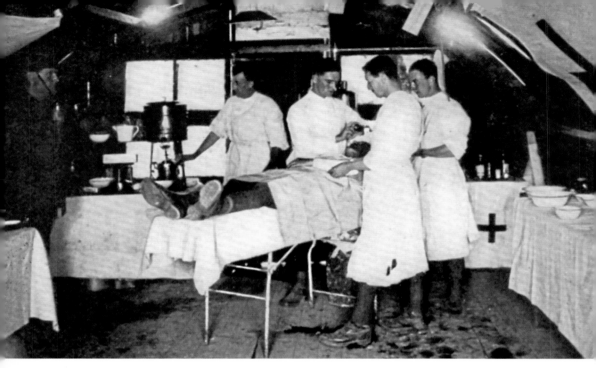

Above: Wounded soldiers being operated on by surgeons in a field ambulance. (Courtesy of Jonathan Reeve b119pl75)

Below: Wounded soldiers being tended to by nurses in a casualty clearing station. (Courtesy of Jonathan Reeve b119pl76)

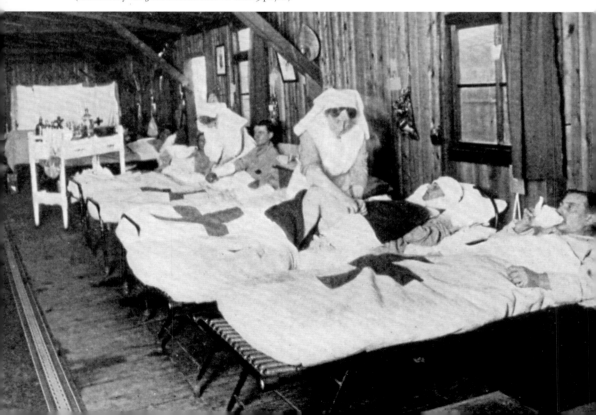

on his stretcher; he was hit in the jaw, the arms, and the hands, but he calmly took out his pipe, placed it in his blood-stained mouth, and started smoking. I was talking to the officer of the Ks, when he suddenly fell to groaning, and rolled over on to my stretcher. I tried to comfort him, but words were of no avail. A doctor came along, asked a few questions, and examined the wound, just a small hole in the pit of the stomach; but he looked serious enough about it. The stretcher was lifted up and its tortured occupant borne away behind the screen for an operation. That was the last I saw of a very plucky young fellow. I ate some bread and jam, and drank some tea doled out liberally all down the two lines of stretchers, for another line had formed by now.

My turn came at last, and I was carried off to a table behind the screen, where the wound was probed, dressed, and bandaged tightly, and I had a foretaste of the less pleasant side of hospital life. There were two Army nurses at work on a case next to mine – the first English women I had seen since I returned from leave six months before. My wound having been dressed, I was almost immediately taken out and put into a motor-lorry. There must have been about nine of us, three rows of three, on the floor of that lorry. I did not find it comfortable, though the best had been done under the circumstances to make it so; neither did the others, many of whom were worse wounded than myself, judging by the groans which arose at every jolt.

We turned down a road leading to the station. Groups of peasants were standing in the village street and crying after us: 'Ah! Les pauvres blessés! Les pauvres Anglais blessés!' These were the last words of gratitude and sympathy that the kind peasants could give us. We drew up behind other cars alongside the hospital train, and the engine driver looked round from polishing his engine and watched us with the wistful gaze of one to whom hospital train work was no longer a

Detail from a contemporary British First World War propaganda poster. (Courtesy of Jonathan Reeve f238)

novelty. 'Walking wounded' came dribbling up by ones and twos into the station yard, and were directed into sitting compartments.

The sun was in my eyes, and I felt as if my face was being scorched. I asked an RAMC NCO, standing at the end of the wagon, to get me something to shade my eyes. Then occurred what I felt was an extremely thoughtful act on the part of a wounded man. A badly wounded lance-corporal, on the other side of the lorry, took out his handkerchief and stretched it over to me. When I asked him if he was sure that he did not want it, he insisted on my taking it. It was dirty and blood-stained, but saved me much discomfort, and I thanked him profusely. After about ten minutes our stretchers were hauled out of the lorry. I was borne up to the officers' carriage at the far end of the train. It was a splendidly equipped compartment; and when I found myself between the sheets of my berth, with plenty of pillows under me, I felt as if I had definitely got a stage nearer to England. Someone behind me called my name, and, looking round, I saw my old friend MW, whose party I had nearly run into the night before in that never-to-be-forgotten communication trench, Woman Street. He told me that he had been hit in the wrist and leg. Judging by his flushed appearance, he had something of a temperature.

More wounded were brought or helped in – men as well as officers – till the white walls of the carriage were lined with blood-stained, mud-covered khaki figures, lying, sitting, and propped up in various positions.

The medical officer in charge of the train came round and asked us what we should like to drink for dinner.

'Would you like whisky and soda, or beer, or lemonade?' he questioned me. This sounded pleasant to my ears, but I only asked for a lemonade.

As the train drew out of the station, one caught a last glimpse of warfare – an aeroplane, wheeling round in the evening sky amongst a swarm of telltale smoke puffs, the explosions of 'Archie' shells.

Above: Detail from a poster by the Welsh artist Frank Brangwyn. (Courtesy of the Library of Congress)

Opposite British Tommies in a front-line trench. (Courtesy of Library of Congress)

ABOUT THE AUTHOR

Edward Liveing was a twenty-year-old junior infantry officer when he led his platoon of the County of London Regiment from the trenches on the Somme in the third wave at Gommecourt at 7.30 a.m. plus 45 seconds on 1 July 1916. He worked for the BBC after the war and died in 1963.